MW00474684

THIS JOURNAL BELONGS TO:

____

PAPERLUSH

PRESS

PAPERLUSH

PRESS